BOA
EDITIONS
LIMITED

The reprinting of this book was made possible
by a generous donation from the physicians and staff
of Borg Imaging Group of Rochester, New York

The Terrible Stories

Poems by
LUCILLE CLIFTON

■

BOA Editions, Ltd. ■ Rochester, New York

LC #: 96–84152

ISBN: 1–880238–37–3 paper

01 02 03 8 7 6 5 4 3

Publication of this book was made possible by a grant from
the Eric Mathieu King Fund of The Academy of American Poets.
Publications by BOA Editions, Ltd.—
a not-for-profit corporation under section 501 (c) (3)
of the United States Internal Revenue Code—
are made possible also with the assistance of grants from
the Literature Program of the New York State Council on the Arts,
the Literature Program of the National Endowment for the Arts,
the Lannan Foundation,
the Sonia Raiziss Giop Charitable Foundation,
the Ames-Amzalak Charitable Trust,
the Rochester Area Foundation Community Arts Fund
administered by the Arts & Cultural Council for Greater Rochester,
the County of Monroe, NY, and Pat and Michael Wilder
and other individual supporters.

Cover Art: Harriet Tubman Series, No. 10, 1939–40 casein tempura
on gessoed hardboard, 17 7/8" x 12", by Jacob Lawrence,
Hampton University Museum, Hampton, Virginia.
Cover Design: Daphne Poulin-Stofer
Author Photo: Rollie McKenna
Typesetting: Richard Foerster
Manufacturing: McNaughton & Gunn, Lithographers
BOA Logo: Mirko

"Shadows" and "Lorena" first appeared in The Paris Review.

Lines from House of Light by Mary Oliver. Copyright © 1990 by Mary
Oliver. Reprinted by permission of Beacon Press, Boston.

BOA Editions, Ltd.
Steven Huff, Publisher
Richard Garth, Chair, Board of Directors
A. Poulin, Jr., President & Founder (1976–1996)
260 East Avenue
Rochester, NY 14604

www.boaeditions.org

The Terrible Stories

for marilyn marlow

contents

telling our stories

the fox came every evening to my door
asking for nothing. my fear
trapped me inside, hoping to dismiss her
but she sat till morning, waiting.

at dawn we would, each of us,
rise from our haunches, look through the glass
then walk away.

did she gather her village around her
and sing of the hairless moon face,
the trembling snout, the ignorant eyes?

child, i tell you now it was not
the animal blood i was hiding from,
it was the poet in her, the poet and
the terrible stories she could tell.

■

1. A Dream of Foxes

fox

. . . The foxes are hungry, who could blame them
for what they do? . . .
                    —*"Foxes in Winter"*
                    Mary Oliver

who
can blame her for hunkering
into the doorwells at night,
the only blaze in the dark
the brush of her hopeful tail,
the only starlight
her little bared teeth?

and when she is not satisfied
who can blame her for refusing to leave,
for raising the one paw up and barking,
Master Of The Hunt, why am i
not feeding, not being fed?

■

the coming of fox

one evening i return
to a red fox
haunched by my door.

i am afraid
although she knows
no enemy comes here.

next night again
then next then next
she sits in her safe shadow

silent as my skin bleeds
into long bright flags
of fur.

■

dear fox

it is not my habit
to squat in the hungry desert
fingering stones, begging them
to heal, not me but the dry mornings
and bitter nights.
it is not your habit
to watch. none of this
is ours, sister fox.
tell yourself that anytime now
we will rise and walk away
from somebody else's life.
any time.

■

leaving fox

so many fuckless days and nights.
only the solitary fox
watching my window light
barks her compassion.
i move away from her eyes,
from the pitying brush
of her tail
to a new place and check
for signs. so far
i am the only animal.
i will keep the door unlocked
until something human comes.

■

one year later

what if,
then,
entering my room,
brushing against the shadows,
lapping them into rust,
her soft paw extended,
she had called me out?
what if,
then,
i had reared up baying,
and followed her off
into vixen country?
what then of the moon,
the room, the bed, the poetry
of regret?

■

a dream of foxes

in the dream of foxes
there is a field
and a procession of women
clean as good children
no hollow in the world
surrounded by dogs
no fur clumped bloody
on the ground
only a lovely line
of honest women stepping
without fear or guilt or shame
safe through the generous fields

■

2. From the Cadaver

amazons

when the rookery of women
warriors all
each cupping one hand around
her remaining breast

daughters of dahomey
their name fierce on the planet

when they came to ask
who knows what you might have
to sacrifice   poet   amazon
there is no choice

then when they each
with one nipple lifted
beckoned to me
five generations removed

i rose
and ran to the telephone
to hear
    cancer   early detection   no
    mastectomy   not yet

there was nothing to say
my sisters swooped in a circle dance
audre was with them and i
had already written this poem

■

lumpectomy eve

all night i dream of lips
that nursed and nursed
and the lonely nipple

lost in loss and the need
to feed that turns at last
on itself   that will kill

its body for its hunger's sake
all night i hear the whispering
the soft

    love calls you to this knife
    for love   for love

all night it is the one breast
comforting the other

■

consulting the book of changes: radiation

each morning you will cup
your breast in your hand
then cover it and ride
into the federal city.

    if there are no cherry blossoms
    can there be a cherry tree?

you will arrive at the house
of lightning. even the children there
will glow in the arms of their kin.

    where is the light in one leaf
    falling?

you will wait to hear your name,
wish you were a child with kin,
wish some of the men you loved
had loved you.

    what is the splendor of one breast
    on one woman?

you will rise to the machine.
if someone should touch you now
his hand would flower.

after, you will stop to feed yourself.
you have always had to feed yourself.

    will i begin to cry?

if you do, you will cry forever.

■

1994

i was leaving my fifty-eighth year
when a thumb of ice
stamped itself hard near my heart

you have your own story
you know about the fear the tears
the scar of disbelief

you know that the saddest lies
are the ones we tell ourselves
you know how dangerous it is

to be born with breasts
you know how dangerous it is
to wear dark skin

i was leaving my fifty-eighth year
when i woke into the winter
of a cold and mortal body

thin icicles hanging off
the one mad nipple weeping

have we not been good children
did we not inherit the earth

but you must know all about this
from your own shivering life

■

scar

we will learn
to live together.

i will call you
ribbon of hunger
and desire
empty pocket flap
edge of before and after.

and you
what will you call me?

woman i ride
who cannot throw me
and i will not fall off.

■

hag riding

why
is what i ask myself
maybe it is the afrikan in me
still trying to get home
after all these years
but when i wake to the heat of morning
galloping down the highway of my life
something hopeful rises in me
rises and runs me out into the road
and i lob my fierce thigh high
over the rump of the day and honey
i ride   i ride

■

down the tram

hell is like this   first stone
then rock so wonderful
you forget you have no faith
some pine   some scrub brush
just enough to clench green
in the air
yes   it is always evening
there are stars   there is sky
you stand there silent
in the long approach
watching as caverns
tense into buildings
wondering who could live here
knowing whatever they have done
they must be beautiful

■

rust

we don't like rust,
it reminds us that we are dying.
—Brett Singer

are you saying that iron understands
time is another name for God?

that the rain-licked pot is holy?
that the pan abandoned in the house

is holy? are you saying that they
are sanctified now, our girlhood skillets

tarnishing in the kitchen?
are you saying we only want to remember

the heft of our mothers' handles,
their ebony patience, their shine?

■

from the cadaver

for bill palmer

the arm you hold up
held a son   he became
taller than his father
if he is watching there
in my dim lit past
let him see
what a man comes to
doctor or patient
criminal or king
pieces of baggage
cold in a stranger's hand

■

3. A Term in Memphis

shadows

in the latter days
you will come to a place
called memphis
there you will wait for awhile
by the river mississippi
until you can feel the shadow
of another memphis and another
river. nile.

wake up girl.
you dreaming.

the sign may be water or fire
or it may be the black earth
or the black blood under the earth.
or it may be the syllables themselves
coded to you from your southern kin.

wake up girl.
i swear you dreaming.

memphis.
capital of the old kingdom
of ancient egypt at the apex
of the river across from
the great pyramids.
nile. born in the mountains
of the moon.

wake up girl,
this don't connect.

wait there.
in the shadow of your room
you may see another dusky woman

weakened by too much loss.
she will be dreaming a small boat
through centuries of water
into the white new world.
she will be weaving garments
of neglect.

wake up girl.
this don't mean nothing.

meaning is the river
of voices. meaning
is the patience of the moon.
meaning is the thread
running forever in shadow.

girl girl wake up.
somebody calling you.

■

slaveships

loaded like spoons
into the belly of Jesus
where we lay for weeks for months
in the sweat and stink
of our own breathing
Jesus
why do you not protect us
chained to the heart of the Angel
where the prayers we never tell
and hot and red
as our bloody ankles
Jesus
Angel
can these be men
who vomit us out from ships
called Jesus   Angel   Grace Of God
onto a heathen country
Jesus
Angel
ever again
can this tongue speak
can these bones walk
Grace Of God
can this sin live

■

entering the south

i have put on my mother's coat.
it is warm and familiar
as old fur
and i can hear hushed voices
through it.   too many
animals have died
to make this.   the sleeves
coil down toward my hands
like rope.   i will wear it
because she loved it
but the blood from it pools
on my shoulders
heavy and dark and alive.

■

the mississippi river empties into the gulf

and the gulf enters the sea and so forth,
none of them emptying anything,
all of them carrying yesterday
forever on their white tipped backs,
all of them dragging forward tomorrow.
it is the great circulation
of the earth's body, like the blood
of the gods, this river in which the past
is always flowing. every water
is the same water coming round.
everyday someone is standing on the edge
of this river, staring into time,
whispering mistakenly:
only here. only now.

■

old man river

everything elegant
but this water

tables set with crystal
at the tea shop

miss lady patting her lips
with linen

horses pure stock
negras pure stock

everything clear
but this big muddy

water

don't say nothin'
must know somethin'

■

Beckwith found guilty of shooting Medgar
Evers in the back, killing him in 1963.
—newspaper 2/94

the son of medgar
will soon be
older than medgar

he came he says
to show in this courtroom
medgar's face

the old man sits
turned toward his old wife
then turns away

he is sick
his old wife sighs
he is only a sick old man

medgar isn't
wasn't
won't be

■

auction street

for angela mcdonald

consider the drum.
consider auction street
and the beat
throbbing up through our shoes,
through the trolley
so that it rides as if propelled
by hundreds, by thousands
of fathers and mothers
led in a coffle
to the block.

consider the block,
topside smooth as skin
almost translucent like a drum
that has been beaten
for the last time
and waits now to be honored
for the music it has had to bear.
then consider brother moses,
who heard from the mountaintop:
take off your shoes,
the ground you walk is holy.

■

memphis

. . . at the river i stand,
guide my feet, hold my hand

i was raised
on the shore
of lake erie
e is for escape

there are more s'es
in mississippi
than my mother had
sons

this river never knew
the kingdom of dahomey

the first s
begins in slavery
and ends in y
on the bluffs

of memphis
why are you here
the river wonders
northern born

looking across from buffalo
you look into canada   toronto
is the name of the lights
burning at night

the bottom of memphis
drops into the nightmare
of a little girl's fear
in fifteen minutes

they could be here
i could be there
mississippi
not the river   the state

schwerner
and chaney
and goodman

medgar

schwerner
and chaney
and goodman
and medgar

my mother had one son
he died gently near lake erie

some rivers flow back
toward the beginning
i never learned to swim

will i float or drown
in this memphis
on the mississippi river

what is this southland
what has this to do with egypt
or dahomey
or with me

so many questions
northern born

■

what comes after this

water earth fire air
i can scarcely remember
gushing down through my mother
onto the family bed
but the dirt of eviction
is still there
and the burning bodies of men
i have tried to love

through the southern blinds
narrow memories enter the room
i had not counted on ice
nor clay nor the uncertain hiss
of an old flame   water earth fire
it is always unexpected and
i wonder what is coming
after this   whether it is air
or it is nothing

■

blake

saw them glittering in the trees,
their quills erect among the leaves,
angels everywhere. we need new words
for what this is, this hunger entering our
loneliness like birds, stunning our eyes into rays
of hope. we need the flutter that can save
us, something that will swirl across the face
of what we have become and bring us grace.
back north, i sit again in my own home
dreaming of blake, searching the branches
for just one poem.

■

4.   In the Meantime

evening and my dead once husband
rises up from the spirit board
through trembled air   i moan
the names of our wayward sons
and ask him to explain   why
i fuss like a fishwife   why
cancer and terrible loneliness
and the wars against our people
and the room glimmers as if washed
in tears and out of the mist a hand
becomes flesh and i watch
as its pointing fingers spell

it does not help to know

■

memory

ask me to tell how it feels
remembering your mother's face
turned to water under the white words
of the man at the shoe store. ask me,
though she tells it better than i do,
not because of her charm
but because it never happened
she says,
no bully salesman swaggering,
no rage, no shame, none of it
ever happened.
i only remember buying you
your first grown up shoes
she smiles. ask me
how it feels.

■

my sanctified grandmother
spoke in tongues
dancing the syllables
down the aisle.

she leaned on light
as she sashayed through
the church hall conversing
with angels.

only now, grown away
from embarrassment,
only now do i beseech her,

i, who would ask the seraphim
to speak to me in my own words:

grandmother
help them to enter
my mouth.   teach me
to lean on understanding.
not my own.   theirs.

■

lee

my mother's people
belonged to the lees
my father would say
then spout a litany
of names   old lighthorse harry
old robert e

my father
who lied on his deathbed
who knew the truth
but didn't always choose it
who saw himself an honorable man

was proud of lee
that man of honor
praised by grant and lincoln
worshipped by his men
revered by the state of virginia
which he loved almost as much
as my father did

it may have been a lie
it may have been
one of my father's tales
if so there was an honor in it
if he was indeed to be
the child of slaves
he would decide himself
that proud old man

i can see him now
chaining his mother to lee

■

album

this lucky old man
is my father.   he is
waving and walking away
from damage he has done.
he is dressed in his good
grey hat, his sunday suit.
he knows himself to be
a lucky man.

today
is his birthday somewhere.
he is ninety.
what he has forgotten
is more than i have seen.
what i have forgotten
is more than i can bear.
he is my father,
our father,
and all of us still love him.
i turn the page, marveling,
jesus christ
what a lucky old man!

■

what did she know, when did she know it

in the evenings
what it was the soft tap tap
into the room   the cold curve
of the sheet arced off
the fingers sliding in
and the hard clench against the wall
before and after
all the cold air   cold edges
why the little girl never smiled
they are supposed to know everything
our mothers   what did she know
when did she know it

■

in the same week

for samuel sayles, jr., 1938–1993

after the third day
the fingers of your folded hands
must have melted together
into perpetual prayer.
it was hot and buffalo.
nothing innocent could stay.

in the same week
stafford folded his tongue
and was gone. nothing
innocent is safe.

the frailty of love
falls from the newspaper
onto our bedroom floor
and we walk past not noticing.
the end of something simple
is happening here,

something essential. brother,
we burned you into little shells
and stars. we hold them hard,
attend too late to each,
mourn every necessary bit.
the angels shake their heads.
too little and too late.

■

heaven

my brother is crouched at the edge
looking down.
he has gathered a circle of cloudy
friends around him
and they are watching the world.

i can feel them there, i always could.
i used to try to explain to him
the afterlife,
and he would laugh. he is laughing now,

pointing toward me. "she was my sister,"
i feel him say,
"even when she was right, she was wrong."

■

lorena

it lay in my palm soft and trembled
as a new bird and i thought about
authority and how it always insisted
on itself, how it was master
of the man, how it measured him, never
was ignored or denied and how it promised
there would be sweetness if it was obeyed
just like the saints do, like the angels,
and i opened the window and held out my
uncupped hand. i swear to god,
i thought it could fly

■

in the meantime

Poem ending with a line from The Mahabharata, *quoted at the time of the first atomic blast.*

the Lord of loaves and fishes
frowns as the children of
Haiti Somalia Bosnia Rwanda Everyhere
float onto the boats of their bellies
and die   in the meantime
someone who is not hungry sits to dine

we could have become
fishers of men
we could have been
a balm
a light
we have become
not what we were

in the mean time
that split apart with the atom
all roads began to lead
to these tables
these hungry children
this time
and

I am become Death   the destroyer of worlds.

■

5.   From the Book of David

for anne caston

dancer

i have ruled
for forty years,
seven in hebron
thirty-three in jerusalem.

i have lain under the stars
and dreamed of foreign women.
i have dreamed my legs around them,
dancing.

some nights,
holding them in the dream,
i would feel us
swallowed by the sky.

lately i have begun to bed
with virgins,
their round breasts warm
to an old man.

i hold my seed
still plentiful as stars.
it is not my time.

somewhere something is choosing.
i can feel it dancing in me,
something to do with
virgins and with stars.

i am grown old and full of days.
my thighs are trembling.
what will the world remember,
what matters to time,
i wonder,
the dancer or the dance?

■

son of jesse

my father had eight sons
seven for keeping

somewhere there is a chronicle
naming my mother

how could i be womantrue
dancing in a house of men

even when i gathered
foreign wives and concubines

i would tend them as i tended
sheep

but when i ripped my robe
and wailed and wept upon the earth

i was grieving for men and i knew it
for my Lord my brothers fathers sons

■

david has slain his ten thousands

i would rise from my covering
and walk at night
to escape the ten thousand
bloody voices

yet i am a man
after God's own heart

when i hung the hands
of my enemy in the square
they came to clutch my dreams
at night

what does He love,
my wrath or my regret?

■

to michal

Michal . . . looked through a window and saw
King David leaping and dancing before the
Lord; and she despised him in her heart.
                              —II Samuel 6:16

moving and moaning
under our coverings
i could only guess
what women know
but wife
in the open arms of God
i became man and woman
filling and emptying
all at once
and oh the astonishment
of seed
dancing on the ground
as i leaped and turned
surrendering
not what i had withheld from you
but michal from myself.

■

enemies

for wayne karlin

evening.
i creep
into the tent
of saul.

for his sake
i have learned
the taste of blood.
in battle
i would drink his
and he mine.

we have become
enemies

yet here
he is an old man
sleeping
or my father.

i will remove
his armaments
his sword
his shield.

come morning
he will know himself
naked but alive

and i will remember
myself also. david.
the poet david.

■

beloved

jonathan the son of saul
did love me
and michal the daughter of saul
did love me
and israel and judah all
and honey was heaped upon my head
and the sword of goliath the giant
was given into my hand
and every harp and timbrel sang with
what doth thy soul desire
and i did not know

until one eventide i walked out
onto the roof of the king's house

■

bathsheba

how it was   it was
as if all of the blood in my body
gorged
into my loin
so that even my fingers grew stiff
but cold
and the heat of my rod
was my only burning
desire
desire my only fire
and whether i loved her
i could not say but
i wanted her whatever she was
whether a curse
or the wife of uriah

■

the prophet

came to me
with a poor man's tale
of his one ewe lamb
sworn to him by seven
pieces of gold

and a tale of the greed
of a rich man
hungry for not his own
supper
who stole that lamb

and i in my arrogance
did swear by the fate
of my house and my kingdom
vengeance

oh the crack in my heart
when the prophet tolled
david
thou art the man

■

oh absolam my son my son

even as i turned myself from you
i longed to hold you oh
my wild haired son

running in the wilderness away
from me from us
into a thicket you could not foresee

if you had stayed
i feared you would kill me
if you left i feared you would die

oh my son
my son
what does the Lord require

■

david, musing

it was i who faced the lion and the bear
who gathered the five smooth stones
and the name of the first was hunger
and the name of the second was faith
and the name of the third was lyric
and passion the fourth and the fifth
was the stone of my regret   it was hunger
that brought the gore of the giant's head
into my hand
the others i fastened under my tongue
for later   for her   for israel   for my sons

■

what manner of man

if i am not singing to myself
to whom then?   each sound, each word
is a way of wondering that first
brushed against me in the hills
when i was an unshorn shepherd boy.
each star that watched my watching then
was a mouth that would not speak.

what is a man? what am i?

even when i am dancing now i am dancing
myself onto the tongue of heaven
hoping to move into some sure
answer from the Lord.
how can this david love himself,
be loved (i am singing and spinning now)
if he stands in the tents of history
bloody skull in one hand, harp in the other?

■

about the author

Lucille Clifton is Distinguished Professor of Humanities at St. Mary's College of Maryland. She has received many fellowships, awards, and distinctions for her poetry collections and children's books, including the Shelley Memorial Prize, the Charity Randall Citation, and an Emmy Award from the American Academy of Television Arts and Sciences. She is the only author to have two books of poetry chosen as finalists for the Pulitzer Prize in one year: *Good Woman: Poems and a Memoir 1969–1980* and *Next: New Poems,* both from BOA, in 1988. These were followed by *Quilting: Poems 1987–1990* (BOA, 1991), and *The Book of Light* (Copper Canyon, 1993). She lives in Columbia, Maryland.

■

BOA EDITIONS, LTD.

AMERICAN POETS CONTINUUM SERIES